U. S. POST OFFICE

BETHLEHEM
GA. --- 30620

GEO

THE · H

By Bill Weems

For Prisca,
Will and Prisca

Photographs, opening pages:
The old Bethlehem Post Office;
The Boneyard, Wassaw Island;
Scenes of Ty Ty—The outer pasture,
Storm light in the cornfield,
Checking the crops;
The Candler Creek swimming hole,
near Gillsville;
Sunrise on the beach, St. Simons Island;
Atlanta skyline.

Designed by Will Hopkins and
Ira Friedlander/Will Hopkins Group.
Design Assistants:
R. LaClaire Rudd and Ingrid von Werz.
Copy Editor: Stephen Brewer.
Type set by Lettra Graphics.
Printed by Rapoport Printing Corp.

Library of Congress Catalog Card Number:
79-88960   ISBN: 0-9603030-1-4

INTRODUCTION

THERE were times while I was on the road when miles became blurs and places nameless. I always managed to remember the people, even though I might've had to dig a bit to come up with their names. Fortunately, there were not too many of these periods of saturation and fatigue, but when they occurred, I felt their impact right down to my dusty shoes. You see, Georgia is big, very big—huge, in fact! To continually travel from one place to another, one mountain to the next, one sea island to another, initiates the accumulation not only of miles, but of visual and emotional images as well. It is difficult to say which of the two I can digest more of before my vision blurs, my mind gets numb and my feet start to drag. When such times occurred during my odysseys around the state, I would just quit for awhile. Either I would go and be with my family, or I would settle myself in a hotel or motel with all the conveniences, and just sort of recuperate for awhile.

In looking back on these enforced periods of calm, I realize that what I was really doing was not just resting, but perhaps even more important, digesting. I then would have time to consider the thoughts some farmer shared with me, or to begin to enjoy the feelings produced by having been "adopted" by a loving family in Tiger Mountain. I would reflect back on the deeply etched face of a man who hunts and catches wild boar bare-handed in the Okefenokee Swamp. I suppose I now better understand why those folks who eat lavish, very rich meals take a long time between courses and stretch out the meal over an entire day or night. It's the same kind of problem— digestion.

I feast on images—on visual sights and signs from the world around me. Food, to be sure, plays an important role during the course of my travels. But for me there is an even more lasting banquet—the one my eyes savor and record. That for me is the real feast. I don't need drugs or weeds or anything special to get high. I just open my eyes and walk around for awhile and sooner or later it happens. The light shifts, softens and becomes warm; or one human being touches another in a special way. Or perhaps it will be the way several canoes lie next to dark, deep-running water; or how a strong, calloused man tenderly holds a wiggling, newly born creature. It's usually this subtle or generally unnoticed event that will trigger a process in me that

makes my soul swell and my visual taste buds sharpen. Such things never lose their grandeur for me. Sometimes during a particularly nice sunrise I shout for joy (a real mood-breaker for those around me). Or if I am alone—all alone—in a wild or very beautiful place, my palms become moist and the blood rushes about inside of me and I get high, just plain high, from being there. If I have someone with me to share it with, all the better.

You might well wonder what all this emotional carrying-on has to do with Georgia and this book. That is certainly a fair question, but the answer doesn't seem to be an easy one for me. I suppose the best way to respond is to repeat what I said a few moments ago: If I have someone with me to share it with, all the better. This book is about sharing. It is my attempt to share with you, or anyone else who gives a whit or is even curious about Georgia and its people, some of my experiences and impressions gathered during my journeys throughout the state.

I had no idea what I would find when I first began photographing the people, the towns and the landscape of Georgia. In the end I was astonished at the deeply ingrained gentility and warmth of the people as well as the incredible variety and beauty of the land. One photograph after the other, the images began to weave a sort of tapestry-like picture of contemporary Georgia. And like other tapestries, ancient and new, the images tell a story of a people and their place in time—of culture, of family, of work, of lots of things. There are many different stories that could be told.

I'm lucky, I guess. I have a job and a life that occasionally allow me to go off and spend months exploring, questioning, looking. If one fork of the road seems just a bit more interesting than the other, off I go in search of whatever is beyond the bend. An interesting house or person will call an immediate halt to my journey and initiate hellos and howdy-dos. The ensuing chat might take five minutes, or five days, and usually leads to still another fork in the road. If I am sorry about anything, it is that I am only me—just one person—and have to begrudgingly limit myself to exploring one road at a time. One might wisely ask just what I'm doing out on those roads to begin with. Why spend so long looking into every corner of the state? Why take so many darn pictures? Again, obvious questions with less obvious answers. But if you really want to know, step back with me to 1943, the year I was born in Atlanta.

Those early memories of my years in Atlanta are sweet, short and dislocated. My neighborhood around the family home had almost everything a kid could want. My playground was the real briar patch at Joel Chandler Harris's home nearby; the corner drugstore had a zillion comics and a lax reading policy.

My brother and I often rode the bus downtown to visit the Fox or to shop with my mother and grandmother. Atlanta was low key then—but an exciting place to begin growing. My father had died two months before my birth, but family life in my grandparents' home was warm and friendly and I didn't feel too much pressure.

It wasn't long, however, before my mom remarried, and soon after my fifth birthday (I was very grown-up for five),

a transfer took us away from Atlanta to the Middle West and then to North Carolina. Maybe those earliest years are the sweetest ones, or maybe life after that just wasn't as pleasant and interesting. Whatever the reason may be, I came to treasure highly the memories of those first five years in Georgia. Occasional trips back to visit both sets of grandparents took place during summer vacations. Brother Marshall and I worked tobacco machines in the fields around Hahira or helped Grandmother Gaddis run one of the local hotel restaurants. We continued to grow with red clay all over our shoes and grandmother's rug. The intense heat of the south Georgia summer seemed comfortable to us and the silver shimmering over the endless rows and mounds of dirt was dreamlike and very beautiful. Once, back in Atlanta, we saw a Tarzan movie six times in a row. Little did we know that the next couple of visits to the home place would each be separated by more than a decade.

All of a sudden I was grown, in the Navy and about to go to Vietnam. Before I left, I married Prisca, a Hungarian immigrant who had gone to high school with me. Not long after my return from the war, we two became three, and several years after that, four. I took my wife back to my early stomping grounds in Atlanta for our first anniversary. I figured that for her to better understand who I was and where I came from, she needed to see my earlier home. We rode the same old merry-go-rounds, stormed Uncle Remus's briar patch and walked rather quickly through the now run-down drugstore. The old neighborhood was a bit seedy looking, but amazing things were happening to the rest of the city. More and more people were streaming into the Atlanta area, and hammers were hard at work everywhere we looked. In the end, I'm sure I got more out of the trip than Prisca did.

Still another decade later, I turned to photography as a way of life. It was a crazy thing to do and made no economic sense, but I was happier after that. My children were now getting quite grown and I was considering taking the entire family back to Georgia for a more extended trip. But I slowly came to realize that no simple visit would satisfy what I really wanted to find out.

I began to do extensive research on the state and found that it had really blossomed since that last visit 10 years before. What had happened in Georgia might well interest the rest of the country, I thought, so I proposed a modern-day Georgia story to *National Geographic* magazine, for which I photograph on a freelance basis. I was delighted when the magazine accepted the proposal and assigned me the story. Now I would be able to investigate what really made Georgia tick, and share it with the magazine's readers.

I photographed for about four months over a period of a year. After the story was published, I returned to Georgia six more times on my own and continued the coverage. In the end, I had traveled approximately 20,000 miles within the state's borders and had visited more than 130 counties. I felt that I had seen and experienced something quite remarkable. My home place ended up being the home place of many other people. Their stories are the most beautiful, diverse and rich, yet personal, sagas I have ever experienced. I ended up being particularly proud to be even a small part of these people and of the land they occupy.

Many countries have far less to offer geographically than does this one state. There is a breathtaking splendor and drama in the mountains; the seashore and swamps exist in a tenuous balance of water and light. In the open plains of middle and south Georgia, the horizon seems endless, the feeling of space exhilarating. One of Georgia's greatest resources is the lushness and character of its land; but perhaps its greatest resource is the people themselves. Wherever I went, I found the people to be open, honest and caring. I experienced, often with members of my family, the warm hospitality of a people who still have a true sense of history and grace.

This book is an outgrowth of my wanting others to see and enjoy what I had just experienced. No place stays the same forever. Buildings rise and fall, people come and go and change cannot be denied. All these forces are hard at work in Georgia. But underneath all this hammering and chugging, this striving and stretching, flows a river of continuity which binds the people together in a way that is not easily explained. For there is a feeling among the Georgian people that doesn't seem to have changed much in decades upon decades. Somehow there is a feeling generated when a people have a sense of their boundaries and an actual first-hand feeling of their soil. It is the kind of thing that bonds strangers together and gives them a willingness to seek a common ground. That ground is Georgia, the home place.— Bill Weems

A LAND IN TIME

EORGIANS are a colorful and distinctive group of Americans, born of a unique set of historical processes and geographical circumstances. They exhibit their distinctiveness in countless ways, as they have for two-and-one-half centuries since their earliest settlement was established at Savannah, near the Atlantic coast, as Britain's most southerly American outpost.

Historically, this distinctiveness appears to have stemmed from at least two factors. One was the tension resulting from the elaborate English plan for the settlement of the colony and from the practical solutions that had to be worked out on the spot by settlers in an alien and unknown land.

Another factor was the scale of the frontier challenges confronting Georgians. Even today, Georgia is the largest state east of the Mississippi River, larger than such countries as East Germany, Greece, Portugal and England. But until Georgia relinquished claims to its western lands to the new United States, its people thought in terms of an even vaster territory stretching all the way from the Atlantic to the Mississippi River.

Size was only one dimension of the frontier challenge. Georgia's territorial expansion was spread over a longer time span than that of any other state. The Indians surrendered their domain grudgingly and only after the most elaborate and highly formalized bargaining. Thus, for the first full century after Georgia's founding in the 1730s, the frontier advanced in a slow-step march as one area after another was wrested from the reluctant and sometimes bellicose Indian neighbors.

Nor did the frontier as a character-forming experience come to an end with the final expulsion of the Indians. Once acquired, the land had to be tamed and made to yield livelihoods and wealth. Agricultural innovations, technological inventions, new transport systems—all brought Georgians a new kind of frontier experience. In fact, the American frontier experience continued unabated in Georgia until at least the time of the Civil War. In modified forms, it continues to influence the character

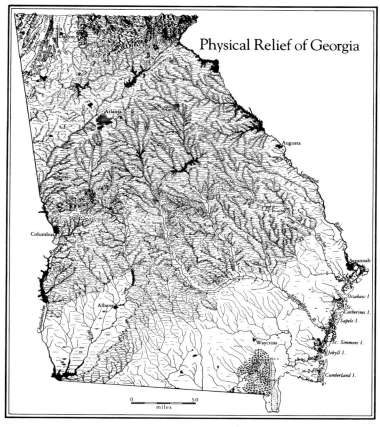

Physical Relief of Georgia

and attitudes of today's rapidly urbanizing and increasingly affluent generation of Georgians.

To understand the history of Georgia, it is also necessary to understand its geography. The best place to begin is a good physiographic map such as the one included here. The cartographer's art and symbolic language provide us with enviably uncluttered views of Georgia's varied land surfaces, which stretch almost 400 miles from the Atlantic's shore in the far southeast to the Appalachian ridges in the far northwest. Also prominent in this view are the courses and directions of the state's rivers and streams—some flowing southeastwardly to the Atlantic and others appearing to cut across the grain and ultimately drain into the Gulf of Mexico. Some drainage can also be seen to flow off toward the north and west to provide a link with the Ohio River system by way of the Tennessee.

It is in the names of Georgia's rivers and streams that one may read a suggestion of the enormous role that Indians played in the centuries preceding the arrival of the whites. These rivers with their euphonious names form an outline of the territorial growth of Georgia because the Indians often used them to mark the limit of the westward spread of the whites. Thus the Savannah, Ogeechee, Canoochee and Altamaha saw the earliest clearings and settlements in their tidal reaches throughout the Coastal Zone. As penetration into the interior proceeded, it followed the valley of the Savannah to the beginning of the strikingly different environments of the upcountry where Augusta was established. For three decades this was Georgia, a scattering of white settlements tenuously established along the coastal islands and marshlands behind and up the floodplain of the Savannah valley to Augusta. In the six decades that followed, the Indians reluctantly retreated to the west and north, making the Ogeechee, Oconee, Ocmulgee, Flint and, finally, the Chattahoochee the boundaries separating white from red Georgia.

Georgia can be divided into three major regions, within

Martha Berry and class of her "industrial school," near Rome, Georgia, ca. 1899.

which terrain, soils, natural vegetation and climate are broadly similar. They are the Coastal Plain, the Piedmont and the Appalachian Mountains.

The first of these, the Coastal Plain, stretches away from the sea toward the interior, rising very gradually from the beaches and tidal marshlands to a belt of higher and hillier land known as the Fall Zone. Along this belt, the very youthful sedimentary rocks and sandy loams of the Coastal Plain begin to give way to the incredibly older rocks that are associated with the Appalachian system stretching from north to south along the eastern side of the North American Continent. The Fall Zone is so named because it is here that rivers flowing from the high interior have descended to and exposed the ancient rocks of the Piedmont, the second of Georgia's great regional divisions.

The Piedmont, underlain by geologically complex ancient rocks, forms a rolling, hilly plateau surface of steeper slopes and heavier clay soils. Here the belt of the Fall Zone stretches across the mid-section of Georgia, from Augusta in the northeast to near Milledgeville on the Oconee, Macon on the Ocmulgee and Columbus on the Chattahoochee. Each of these important Georgia cities owes its existence to the early recognition of the significance of the Fall Zone as the head of river navigation from the sea.

Even earlier, their Fall Zone sites had been occupied and exploited by the Indians, and abandoned Indian villages, agricultural clearings and trail systems added immeasurably to their value as settlement locations. The differences in soils and vegetation found above and below the Fall Zone made it a strategic locale from which an incredibly wide range of plant, animal and mineral resources could be efficiently exploited. Above the Fall Zone, the heavier soils supported a forest cover dominated by nut-bearing hardwood trees such as oak and hickory. Below the Fall Zone, the more-elevated stretches supported seemingly endless pine forests on porous sandy soils that came to be called "Pine Barrens." In the river floodplains, the tough wooded cypress and an assemblage of other water tolerant trees dominated the scene. Near to the coast and on the islands, the majestic live oaks and cedars promised a bonanza in the form of ship timbers. Naval stores—pitch, rosin and turpentine—were to provide the basis for important economic development when the labor, skills and commercial markets became realities.

The Coastal Plain occupies about 60 per cent of modern Georgia's area. The remaining 40 per cent is largely Piedmont, with the northernmost tier dominated by the lofty slopes of the geologically ancient and rounded Appalachian Mountains. The visitor to Atlanta, the state's capital and largest city, is treated to a view of these heights when first approaching the city by air. To the traveler on the ground, the Piedmont merges almost imperceptibly with the mountains as the land becomes higher and hillier, with steeply sloping land coming to clearly dominate the scene. The highest point in Georgia is Brasstown Bald, where the elevation reaches 4,784 feet above sea level.

The natural links for Georgia's three natural divisions are the major rivers, flowing from the highlands to the sea.

Church group,
Savannah area,
ca.1880.
William Wilson
photographer.

Overall, humid, sub-tropical climate prevails, though there is a wide variation in daily weather conditions from one end of the state to another. More than 200 frost-free days guarantee an extremely wide range of agricultural opportunities. Rainfall is high and fairly evenly distributed throughout the year. Snow is known but not frequent on the Piedmont and Coastal Plain. Winter average temperatures are always above 32°F, but daily temperatures often fall well below freezing. A modest ski-slope industry based on the frequent use of snow-making machines has developed in the mountains in recent years.

Whatever the local variations, Georgia is a lush land. The journalist W. G. Cash has written eloquently of the South he loved, and no state better fits his description of the "Southern physical world":

The country is one of extravagant colors, of proliferating foliage and bloom, of flooding yellow sunlight, and, above all perhaps, of haze. Pale blue fogs hang above the valleys in the morning, the atmosphere smokes faintly at midday, and through the long slow afternoon cloud-stacks tower through the iridescent air, blurring every outline and rendering every object vague and problematical. I know that winter comes to the land, certainly. I know there are days when the color and the haze are stripped away and the real stands up in drab and depressing harshness. But these things pass and are forgotten.

The dominant mood, the mood that lingers in the memory, is one of well-nigh drunken reverie—of a hush that seems all the deeper for the far-away mourning of the hounds and the far-away crying of the doves—of such sweet and inexorable opiates as the rich odors of hot earth and pinewood and the perfume of the Magnolia in bloom—of soft languor creeping through the blood and mounting surely to the brain . . . .

Into this lush landscape, more than four centuries ago, moved the first European explorers—probably the band of Spaniards led by Hernando De Soto in 1540. What they found was far from the forest primeval envisioned by some historians. The landscape already bore the marks of centuries of use and modification by the Indians—ecological changes wrought by planting, hunting and, most important, fire. The Indians resorted to burning the forests to encourage the growth of fresh young vegetation and thus provide brouse for the deer that yielded food and the soft, supple hides that would later become the mainstay of trade with the white settlers. The result was open woodland vistas, which many Europeans likened to the wooded parklands they had left at home. Moreover, these and other areas were laced by a skein of trails that formed a network almost as dense as the paved highways of today.

Though De Soto is said to have extorted a modest store of freshwater pearls from a legendary Indian queen in Georgia, the bounty must have paled beside the prodigious treasures of silver and gold being gathered by the Spaniards in their empire farther south. In any event, Spain showed little further interest in the state until the French established a settlement on the St. Johns River just south of Georgia. This development could not be ignored by the Spanish, who needed to protect their vital sea link

Church group,
Savannah area,
ca. 1880.
William Wilson
photographer.

between Cuba and Spain. Along this link passed the fleets of treasure-laden galleons, following the majestic flow of the Gulf Stream north along the length of Florida, Georgia and the Carolinas. The Spanish moved to wipe out the French intrusion in a massacre memorialized in the name of the Matanzas River.

Following the massacre of the French, the Spanish founded their own city of St. Augustine. Florida provided the base from which a vigorous series of Roman Catholic missions spread north along the Georgia coastal islands to the Carolinas in the 16th and 17th centuries. The mission system required large sedentary populations of village-dwelling Indians, and the priests worked hard to encourage Indian agricultural pursuits and animal husbandry—innovations that were to spread into the interior of Georgia and affect the lives of tribal groups who never came into direct contact with the coastal missionaries.

No real threat to the Spanish control of Guale—as her coastal Georgia territory was called—developed until 1670, when the increasingly aggressive British established themselves at Charles Town and began to develop South Carolina. South Carolina Indian traders and freebooters fomented rebellion among the mission Indians and sometimes led direct attacks on the Spanish outposts. Mission after mission was abandoned until the St. Johns River served as the frontier of Spanish-occupied territory. After a century of Spanish mission occupation, the Coastal Zone had become a battleground later to be known as "The Debatable Land," where Carolinians and their Indian allies were replacing the banner of Bourbon Spain with that of Britain. In 1713, the Treaty of Utrecht signaled a resumption of peace between the great powers, but failed to resolve the territorial competition involving Georgia and the rest of southeastern North America.

In the 20 years following the Treaty, a number of British schemes for settling the buffer zone between Carolina and Florida were proposed. Nothing came of these until a group of influential philanthropists began to foster the idea of a new colony in America that could serve as a haven for England's growing population of debtors. A leading spirit in this group was the scion of a well-to-do family, James Edward Oglethorpe, who had won national recognition as chairman of a Parliamentary committee investigating England's jails. Oglethorpe was an experienced soldier who had campaigned widely in Continental wars. In him came together two of the important threads that were to eventuate in the establishment of Georgia: the altruism that saw the new colony as a place of new beginnings for England's deserving poor and the imperial strategy that saw it as a bulwark to guard Carolina's southern flank. The third thread was the economic one of mercantilism. The mercantilists were convinced that a colony in the latitudes south of the Carolinas could produce a valuable range of tropical crops and silk. Early in 1732, the charter for the new colony—named after the reigning King George—was awarded to the 21 incorporated "Trustees for Establishing the Colony of Georgia in America." By the terms of the charter, the colony was to occupy the land between the Savannah and Altamaha rivers and from the heads of those rivers "westward to the

Rosin barrels and stevedores on the Savannah waterfront, ca.1884. William Wilson photographer.

South Seas." After 21 years of administration by the Trustees, the colony was to revert to the Crown.

Prospective settlers were carefully screened because the Trust was making a large grant to each in the form of free passage, equipment and food for the first year, seeds, agricultural implements and a plot of land on which to farm. In the screening process most released debtors were eliminated and Georgia's pioneers came mainly from the ranks of London's tradesmen, artisans and laborers. With Oglethorpe in charge, they arrived at Charlestown in mid-January, 1733 and founded—on the Savannah River about 14 miles from the sea—Georgia's first town and capital, Savannah.

FROM the outset, Georgia was a planned colony in the fullest sense. There is no better evidence of that fact today than the attractive precincts of historic Savannah. Oglethorpe surveyed and laid out the town as an arrangement of straight streets and open squares. It was an urban pattern in which wards of homes would be built around the squares, which could serve a variety of social and commercial purposes. During periods of emergency, the squares could also serve as safe refuges for people and domestic animals from outlying settlements or as encampments for troops. Today the squares are attractive parks providing delightful breaks in Savannah's urban fabric.

Since it was planned that Georgia's settlers should be yeoman farmers rather than absentee plantation operators, they were each allotted only 50 acres of land, broken into three separate parcels. A small town lot was located in one of Savannah's wards. Near the town limits was a garden plot of five acres and, still farther out, a 45-acre farm lot.

During these early years, the most populous community in Georgia comprised the German-speaking protestants who had settled upstream from Savannah around the town of Ebenezer. Most of these Germans came via Salzburg and were known collectively as Salzburgers. Descendants keep their memory alive through Georgia's large Salzburger Society, which still holds its meetings in Ebenezer's handsome pre-Revolutionary church, the only surviving building of the once-flourishing town.

Throughout the period of the Trusteeship, the Salzburgers formed a community apart, strictly controlled by dedicated German clergymen. After some very harrowing early years, their numbers swelled as immigration from Central Europe continued and frontier techniques of farming and animal husbandry were mastered. By the mid-1700s, more Georgians spoke German as a mother tongue

Icehouse interior,
Macon, ca.1890.

25

than English. In the 19th century, the sandy lands surrounding Ebenezer were gradually abandoned by the descendants of the Salzburgers, who increasingly blended with their neighbors and moved to take up the Indian lands of the Piedmont and western Coastal Plain.

The accomplishments of the Georgian colony under the English Trust were many. One of the Trust's earliest enterprises was an experimental botanical garden adjacent to Savannah. Roads were opened and outlying settlements established. And thanks largely to James Oglethorpe's understanding and insight, the colony adopted policies that formed the basis for Georgia's amazingly cordial relationships with the Indians during a period when neighboring South Carolina was often beset by costly Indian warfare on the frontier.

But two provisions of the Trust's ambitious plan for the colony stirred increasing discontent among the settlers. One was the regulation prohibiting the sale of rum and other spirits in Georgia. The other was the prohibition of slavery. To the Trustees, slavery was not only repugnant on moral grounds but also antagonistic to their plan for a Georgia populated by a hard-working yeomanry of small landholders. To the settlers, these ideals flew in the face of economic realities. South Carolina and the other neighboring southern colonies had developed lucrative systems of production on the basis of slave labor. The dispersed landholdings of Georgia were difficult to operate effectively except by the very largest families, and many of the settlers were overwhelmed by the problem of clearing the land in the tropical heat of summer.

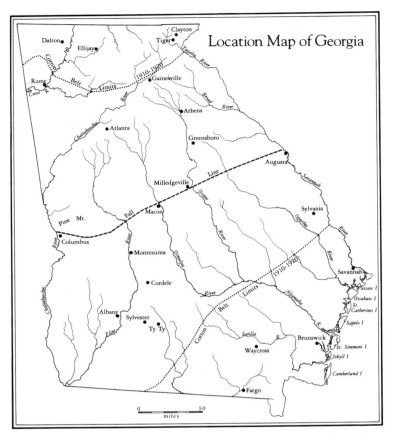

Location Map of Georgia

As settler discontent grew, the Trustees were forced to gradually allow the introduction of both slavery and rum and spirits. Yet even this failed to stem the tide of discontent. The Trust was too far away from the new colony to understand the economics of agricultural and commercial life in an alien land, and the communications links between Georgia and London were too slow for rapid redress of the settlers' complaints. Tensions became so great, in

Girl with cotton,
River Street,
Savannah.

fact, that the Trustees were forced to return the colony's charter to the Crown before the completion of the 21-year term originally granted.

Under royal authority, Georgia prospered. Parliament poured in large infusions of money and, in an effort to attract new settlers, land granting was greatly liberalized. Land tracts essential for plantation-scale agriculture were more easily acquired. Slavery was not only tolerated but also clearly encouraged, since a grantee could expect additional quantities of land proportional to the number of slaves he brought with his family.

A pattern of land occupancy based on rice plantations soon came to dominate Coastal Plain Georgia as it did the Carolinas. With the coming of plantation agriculture, the pace of commerce quickened and a merchant class lent new vigor to Savannah, Sunbury and other settlements. Important among these merchants was Savannah's small community of Jews, who had arrived as early as 1733.

The extraordinarily rapid growth of Georgia as a royal colony is reflected by early population statistics. At the end of its tenure, the Trust reported that Georgia had 2,120 inhabitants. Of these the overwhelming number, 1,700, were white and 420 were black. By the year 1760, there was a total population of almost 10,000, of which more than one-third was black. In 1773, on the eve of the American Revolution, there were about 33,000 inhabitants, of whom 15,000 were black. Slavery was well on its way to becoming the most important economic and social institution in Georgia.

The slaves were concentrated largely in the rice and indigo plantations of the more favored Coastal Plain soils. The typical plantation probably employed 40 to 50 slaves on a landholding of 450 or 500 acres. Aside from slavery, the most prominent social development to grow out of plantation agriculture was the rise of a landed aristocracy. This group, which came to make up about 5 per cent of the population by the time of the Revolution, held more than 20 per cent of the best productive land and over 50 per cent of the slaves. The bulk of the rest of Georgia's citizens were small planters and subsistence farmers. The small planters usually operated farms of some 50 acres with their families and a handful of slaves. The subsistence farmers had even smaller farms and no slaves.

As Georgia's population grew, so did the demand for more Indian land on which to settle. Modest cessions of territory were secured but, as late as the early 1770s, Georgia remained largely a Coastal Plain colony. In only a confined area beyond Augusta were the heavier soils and hardwood forests of the Piedmont included within Georgia's boundary. In this area, just above the Fall Zone, important movements were afoot. It was here that the first ripple of a growing tide of frontiersmen, who considered themselves more Virginians or Carolinians than Britons, were following the long arc of the Piedmont southward. They were a new and different breed of self-reliant pioneers with very few slaves and little love for coastal aristocrats. From their Piedmont homes in Virginia, Maryland and the Carolinas, they brought a very different way of life, which centered on the cultivation of tobacco and corn.

Central City Park,
Macon, ca.1876.

In 1773, the land problem was eased when Georgia's energetic governor, James Wright, secured the permission and cooperation of the royal government in purchasing two huge tracts from the Cherokee and Creek Indians. The Indians, by now entirely dependent on European guns, knives, blankets and clothing, had slipped deeply into debt. Moreover, overhunting by Indians and whites had probably lowered the importance of the lands in question, and the Indians saw a chance of eliminating their debts through the cession. One of the tracts was a vast strip of Coastal Plain stretching between the Ogeechee and the Altamaha Rivers. The other, more important tract was wholly on the Piedmont and stretched north to Hart County on the Savannah River and almost to Athens on the west.

The famous Quaker naturalist William Bartram accompanied the surveyors and Indians engaged in marking the boundary of what became known as the "New Purchase" in the area northwest of Augusta. Here Bartram encountered what he eloquently described as "trees of vast growth which at once spoke its fertility."

The ground is perfectly a level green plain, thinly planted by nature with the most stately forest trees such as the gigantic black oak . . . whose mighty trunks, seemingly of an equal height, appeared like superb columns. To keep within the bounds of truth and reality in describing the magnitude and grandeur of these trees, would I fear fail of credibility; yet, I can assert that many of the black oaks measured eight, nine, ten, and eleven feet diameter five feet above the ground, as we measured several that were above thirty feet girth, and from hence they ascend perfectly straight, with a gradual taper, forty or fifty feet to the limbs. . . .

With such magnificent trees suggesting fertile soils, the New Purchase lands served as a magnet for a flood of new settlers into Georgia via the Piedmont route from the north. For administrative purposes, the new lands were organized as Wilkes County and more than 65,000 acres were sold to the newcomers in the first three months. The lands were not granted free, but had been moderately valued from one to five shillings an acre according to quality. The pioneer families were non-slaveholders who took farm-size tracts of 200 acres or less. They thus blended well with the tobacco- and corn-growing frontiersmen who had preceded them into the Georgia Piedmont a few years before.

In 1775, Georgia joined in the developing American Revolution against British rule. This fact ironically reflected how well the colony had flourished during its two decades under royal administration. Its thriving economic development had bred a spirit of independence and security that was easily fanned into defiance. Not all Georgians abandoned the royal cause. These opponents of the Revolution—known as Tories—drew from a number of groups such as ex-government officeholders, the Anglican clergy, wealthy coastal landowners and merchants, Indian traders and recent immigrants from Britain. Many Salzburgers and upcountry Quakers were loyal to the Crown or remained neutral. Most of the leaders of Revolu-

Idle Hour Farm
cotton field,
Macon, 1894.

tionary Georgia were young, and many were sons of distinguished Tories.

Though Georgia was remote from the formal warfare taking place to the north, bitter civil war raged for much of the period from 1776 to 1782. Many reminders of royal rule were eliminated by the zealous leaders of the new state government. For example, they abandoned the system of parishes that had formed the colony's framework of local government and administration. In the place of names like Christ Church, St. Matthew and St. Andrew Parish, Georgia's new map reflected the counties established to give voters more control of local affairs. These counties bore testament to the Revolutionary spirit with names like Liberty, Wilkes, Richmond, Burke, Effingham, Chatham, Glynn and Camden. All but Liberty were named after British politicians who were notably friendly to colonial causes.

After the Revolution, land once again became Georgia's chief preoccupation. Something approaching 90 or 95 per cent of the territory that now makes up the state still remained under Indian control or was otherwise ungranted. For the first decade after the war, land was granted in much the way it had been in the colonial period. A newly arrived settler or war veteran was issued an authorization for a qualified land surveyor to mark out a tract, which, in the parlance of the day, was granted on the "head right" of the settler and his dependents. Such tracts, in the coastal belt and eastern tier of counties, comprised about two-fifths of today's Georgia and are often called the "head right" landscape. Individual parcels of land here tend to be irregularly shaped. The field boundaries, woodlots, fencelines, lanes and roads of today are a random patchwork quilt reflecting the irregular orientation of the lines marked out by the original surveyors two centuries ago. This same head-right pattern was followed in the settlement of the New Purchase land cessions negotiated with the Cherokee and Creek Indians in the 1780s and 1790s as far west as the Oconee River.

Beyond the Oconee, however, the pattern of survey and settlement reflects the radical new policy of land distribution adopted around 1800. Here and over the whole of western Georgia, the geometry of settlement, in its rectangular regularity, resembles the checkerboard-like landscape of the American Middle West. Georgia's new land policy sought to avoid the speculation and fraud that had marred the head-right system during the 1790s by insuring that family-farm size tracts would pass directly into the hands of owner-occupiers. Large tracts, ranging from 202½ to 490 acres, were laid out in neat rectangles. Then, to distribute this vast domain between the Oconee and Chattahoochee rivers, a number of public lotteries were held between 1804 and 1832. The lucky Georgian who drew a lot had only to pay a few dollars to register his freehold grant. The western three-fifths of Georgia is known to this day as the Land Lottery region. More than any other landscape in the United States, it embodies the ideals of the American Revolution and deserves to be called the landscape of the common man.

The lottery system represented the old Trustee ideal of a frontier compactly settled by yeoman farmers. In another

Tractor driver,
ca.1920.

development reminiscent of Trustee planning, cities were being planned in advance of actual settlement. The legislation drawn up to cover the surveying of each Indian cession also included provisions for carefully planned cities such as Milledgeville, Macon and Columbus. These cities, like Augusta earlier, were sited in the Fall Zone to serve as focal points at the head of river navigation from the seacoast. The pattern of broad, regularly intersecting streets, which continue to make these cities attractive and efficient urban centers, was copied up and down the state as county-seat towns were created to serve the needs of a growing population.

The orgy of land acquisition tended to conceal the inherent tensions in post-Revolutionary Georgia. It is no exaggeration to say the new state was probably well on its way to becoming two states—epitomized by the slave-holding plantation owners of the Coastal Plain and the pioneer tobacco and corn farmers of the Piedmont. They comprised two distinct societies occupying two distinctly different environments; they followed diverging economic paths and were heirs to two radically different social traditions.

Some kind of socio-economic cement was obviously needed to bind these two increasingly disparate ways of life. The cement that would unite the people of Georgia for almost a century and a half—and lend them an indelible character—was cotton. Though cotton was being produced in the late 18th century in neighboring South Carolina, the long staple fiber that grew there was suitable for cultivation only along the coastal margins and islands of Georgia. On the other hand, the upland variety that grew best in Georgia had a short staple fiber, which made the removal of seeds by hand a prohibitively laborious process.

Georgia's cotton problem was solved in 1793 by a young Yankee named Eli Whitney. At the time, Whitney was residing at Mulberry Grove, the plantation near Savannah that had been presented to Revolutionary War General Nathanael Greene by the grateful citizens of Georgia. To draw the short fibers cleanly away from the cotton seeds, Whitney used a saw-toothed disc and thus perfected the cotton gin.

Cotton could now be profitably produced on large plantations by gangs of slaves or on smaller farms by family labor alone. In its versatility it proved to be a great unifying force, helping to weld Georgians of all levels. The Piedmont proved to be cotton's most productive region in the early decades. Within 20 years of Whitney's perfection of the gin, cotton had begun to change dramatically the character of agriculture and life there. Plantations, complete with slaves and landed aristocracy, began to vie with the small subsistence farms, which had heretofore dominated the rolling red clay hills of the region above the Fall Zone. Thus, in the early decades of the 19th century, slavery crystalized into an essential institution of the new Georgia.

With cotton selling at 29 cents a pound in the 1820s, great wealth seemed within the grasp of everyman. Georgia soon became the world's largest producer. Annual output soared to 500,000 bales in 1850 and nearly 750,000

Playing baseball, University of Georgia, Athens, 1893. E. Telamon Cuyler photographer.

in 1860. In her renowned novel, *Gone With the Wind*, Margaret Mitchell vividly evoked this time when cotton was king and a "high tide of prosperity" was rolling across the South.

All of the world was crying out for cotton, and the new land of the County, unworn and fertile, produced it abundantly. Cotton was the heartbeat of the section, the planting and the picking were the diastole and systole of the red earth. Wealth came out of the curving furrows, and arrogance came too—arrogance built on green bushes and the acres of fleecy white. If cotton could make them rich in one generation how much richer they would be in the next.

COTTON, to be sure, was only a segment of Georgia's economy. Wheat, oats, rice and tobacco were also commercially significant crops and indeed, in 1850, some 40 per cent of the state's cultivation was given over to corn production. On the eve of the Civil War, there was also enough industry—iron mills, tanneries, flour mills, machine shops and, of course, textile production—to earn Georgia the sobriquet "Empire State of the South."

Indeed, only a small minority of Georgia's farms were large enough to count as plantations. Of the 62,003 farms listed in the 1860 census, 3,600 had from 500 to 1,000 acres and 902 had more than 1,000 acres. Thus, only about 7 per cent of all the farms in the state possessed anything like the "endless acres" of the plantations described in Margaret Mitchell's novel. Moreover, only about the same small percentage of Georgians controlled the labor of 30 or more slaves. The vast majority of citizens owned few, if any, slaves, and operated farm-size holdings or worked as laborers or artisans.

Nonetheless, it was cotton and the plantation way of life that epitomized the state in the eyes of her own people. The porticoed mansion became the symbol of their aspirations. And Georgia, with more plantations than any other Southern state, had come to epitomize the feeling that the South was a special culture or civilization. Southerners saw this culture as morally and materially superior to that of the North, and imbued with nobler ideals. And they saw slavery as the indispensible underpinning of their way of life. Whether this condition was fact or fiction has concerned generations of economic historians. But Southerners acted as if it were true, and slavery became a central issue in the growing sectional controversy between the South and the North. When the ultimate clash came in the form of the Civil War, most Southerners, slave owners

Samuel Rutherford, "Big Smith," Thomas W. Hardwick, Billie Armstrong, Robert Hunter, University of Georgia, Athens, 1893. E. Telamon Cuyler photographer.

University of Georgia main entrance, Athens, 1893. E. Telamon Cuyler photographer.

or not, joined in the defense of their common heritage and culture.

Some 120,000 Georgians served under the colors of the Confederate States of America against the United States. Obviously, Georgia's blacks, who made up 44 per cent of the state population, were considerably less enthusiastic for the cause of Southern secession from the Union. Most slaves labored on much as they always had. Occasionally, groups of blacks were shifted about to assist in military activities or to escape threats from advancing Union forces. In its last gasp, in March in 1865, the Confederacy moved to recruit blacks into its Army, something the Union Army had been doing for three years.

Union Army coastal attacks and sporadic raids into the state were a prelude for the final and crushing blows that were to flatten Atlanta in the last summer of 1864. In mid-November, General William T. Sherman initiated his infamous "March to the Sea," which cut a 50-mile wide swath across the heartland of the Confederacy. Starting from Atlanta, his marauding army split into two main branches. The left wing moved along the route of the Georgia Railroad to Madison and Milledgeville while the other went overland to the southeast. In their wake, they left a broad belt of near-total destruction. Railroads, bridges, factories, mills and warehouses were relentlessly sought out and destroyed. Even private homes and property, despite orders to the contrary, suffered.

In a little over a month, with Georgia largely destroyed behind him, Sherman marched in to take Savannah. One final arrogant flourish guaranteed his name a prominent place in the chronicle of Southern infamy when he telegraphed President Lincoln: "I beg to present you as a Christmas gift the city of Savannah, with one hundred and fifty heavy guns and plenty of ammunition, also about twenty-five thousand bales of cotton."

With the emancipation of all slaves, three-quarters of Georgia's capital disappeared in a trice. Much of the countryside was laid waste, money and state bonds were worthless, the railroads were torn up and most of Georgia's leaders were either dead or in exile. It was necessary to build a new society and this would have to be done largely from within. The Northern victors looked upon the Confederate States as defeated enemies who required punishment rather than aid in rebuilding their devastated economies. In the harshness of the Reconstruction process, all Georgians could join in a common resentment against the Yankee villains as they could join in a common feeling of nostalgia for the lost cause of the Confederacy. And after economic realities had extinguished the elation first felt by the now politically liberated blacks, they too came to share in what was a regional sense of misfortune. The bonds of personal understanding that had always existed between white and black Georgians expanded through the long decades of economic deprivation shared by the races after the Civil War.

In a sense, Georgians had to face frontier conditions again. New ways had to be found to master the environment, to replace the institution of slavery that had formed the link between land and labor. After experimentation with various contractual arrangements for farm labor, a

Barbecue.

system of paying the worker with some portion of the crop became a generally accepted institution over Georgia and the South at large. Land, labor and capital were brought together through the system known as "sharecropping." Almost invariably, the land and capital were in white hands while labor was largely black.

The new system's chief virtue was that it worked and allowed Georgia's broken agrarian machine to get back into production. A vast pool of uneducated labor, black and white, was mobilized on a land base that remained in the control of a minority group that lacked almost every other form of capital. The average Georgian of both races preferred sharecropping to some alternative form of "wage slavery." Sharecropping, for all its ills, gave the cropper a large degree of control over his day-to-day life. The family became the work unit as the land was broken up into family-farm size units. In the case of Georgia's blacks, this lent a strength to the family that had never existed under slavery. In times of high prices and good harvests, everyone, black and white alike, benefited from the system; in times of depression and natural disaster, both races suffered in unison. Thus, a common identity and kinship with the land cut across the lines of race. This is not, of course, to assert that anything like true economic or social parity existed between the races. The whites were in control. Exploitation of blacks had not ended with the Civil War.

With sharecropping and the other forms of land tenancy that now dominated Southern agriculture came the crop-lien system of credit. In this characteristically Southern system, merchants extended credit for the seed, equipment, fertilizer, food, clothing and other needs of the farmer in return for a lien or first claim on the crop. When harvests were good, everyone might profit, but when they were bad the farmer often fell deeply into debt. He would find his next year's crop twice mortgaged. It is easy to see how some minor mishap, such as personal illness or accident or the vagaries of weather at some crucial period, could trigger a cycle of fiscal collapse. More often than not, price fluctuations in the world cotton market would clamp economic depression on the whole state. While black tenants and poor whites suffered most severely in depressions, there was an overall sense of shared adversity.

Though the landscape of Georgia underwent a profound change after the Civil War as old plantations were broken up into smaller family-farm size units, cotton was still king through boom and bust. Despite depression during the 1890s, more and more was being planted with the total cotton area growing from 3.5 million acres to over 5 million acres in 1916. The World War I period brought a vigorous demand for cotton and price levels rose dramatically. By 1919, Georgia's farmers were receiving 35 cents a pound for their fiber. But the following year, overproduction and a decline in demand combined to bring a catastrophic drop to 17 cents a pound. The Great Depression, which eventually involved the remaining United States and most of the Western World in the 1930s, thus began a decade early in Georgia.

No author has captured the essense of this period better

Reunion, ca.1900.

than Erskine Caldwell in his 1932 novel, *Tobacco Road*. Like *Gone With the Wind*, it has been published in a score of foreign languages and served as the inspiration for an extremely successful motion picture. It could be convincingly argued that the image of Georgia held by the majority of people in the world outside the United States has been derived from one or both of these books. Caldwell's setting is a full 60 years later than Margaret Mitchell's in *Gone With the Wind*, and his characters are representative of the lowest stratum of Georgia's agrarian society in the depths of the Great Depression.

KING Cotton was rocked by Georgia's economic shocks, but it took a final blow from nature to dethrone him once and for all. Cotton's *coup de grace* was delivered by an insect, the boll weevil. The weevil had made its way into the United States from Mexico, first arriving in southern Georgia in 1913. By the early 1920s, it hit like a scourge in some of the state's most productive cotton regions. In the worst-hit pockets, such as Greene County, the boll weevil's impact was so devastating that large numbers of families chose to abandon their farms and leave the region. Between 1920 and 1925, 3.5 million acres of cotton land were abandoned and the number of farms in Georgia fell from 310,132 to 249,095. In one lifetime, Georgians experienced two depression decades and the boll weevil disaster. It is with good cause that the state's older citizens often reveal lingering elements of fatalism and deep-seated cynicism in their character.

Georgia, like the rest of the United States, was led out of the depths of depression by the administration of President Franklin D. Roosevelt. The easy availability of credit it brought was instrumental in undermining the hold of the crop-lien system. Agricultural diversification was greatly encouraged by both state and federal agencies. Peaches and peanuts began to make important contributions to Georgia farm incomes. Both of these crops have come to be key elements in the state's present agricultural system. Tobacco became increasingly important, and livestock rearing and dairying, as well as commercial chicken and egg production, also got underway. In spite of all that was done to diversify the economy and relieve depression during the 1930s, however, Georgia remained overwhelmingly rural, and her citizens earned the meager per capita income of only $317 in 1940.

World War II brought change and a base for renewed prosperity. Thousands of Georgians, white and black, were called into the armed services or sought employment

Family snapshot, near Savannah Beach, ca.1890.

in expanding defense industries. Even more thousands from the far corners of the United States flowed into Georgia for military training. Georgia boasted an Army training establishment second only to that found in Texas. The town of Warner Robins was created to serve the needs of the huge Air Corps base located near Macon. Columbus, Augusta, Atlanta and Savannah, as well as a host of other towns and cities, were dramatically affected by large military bases located nearby. Aircraft, munitions and shipbuilding plants sprang up to provide industrial jobs across the state.

The post-war years saw economic prosperity increase rapidly in Georgia. The 1950 census revealed that for the first time in the state's history, more Georgians were employed in manufacturing and industry than in agriculture. It wouldn't be an exaggeration to see this as marking the entry of the state into the increasingly affluent mainstream of American life. It was in the cities, particularly Atlanta, that the jobs were being created and the largest share of the new wealth was concentrated. And it was in and around the cities that change was most rapid and far reaching. By 1970, more than 60 per cent of Georgia's 4,589,575 people lived in urban settings. The Atlanta metropolitan area loomed overall as the home of about half of these urban dwellers. Moreover, relatively few of Georgia's rural dwellers actually worked on farms. Rather, they tended to live in the country and work in towns, to which they commuted over the greatly improved highway network.

Agriculture has come to be heavily mechanized with fewer and fewer farm workers producing more and more. In the 20 years from 1949 to 1969, for example, the number of farm families in Georgia dropped from 220,000 to 47,000. Those remaining on the farm tended to specialize. Poultry, for example, became Georgia's single most important agricultural undertaking, accounting for about one-third of all farm income. The traditional row crops—corn, cotton and tobacco—had been joined by soybeans and peanuts to produce about another one-third. Livestock, dairying and fruit and other specialty productions accounted for the remaining one-third of farm income in 1970. The most visible result of these dramatic changes in Georgia's pattern of agriculture is immediately apparent in the vast area of the state covered in forests. Rather than "Peach State," Georgia now deserves the nickname "Pine State," in recognition of the fact that 70 per cent of the state's area is devoted to forests that are largely pine. Not since the beginning of the 18th century has so much of Georgia been under tree and grass cover. The pine forests are also one of the state's important resources—the basis for very lucrative paper, lumber, plywood and naval stores industries.

There can be no doubt that the present generation of Georgians stands squarely in the midst of the urban-industrial way of life. It is a way of life full of promise on the one hand and problems on the other. In the photographs of this book both promise and problems are discernible. So too are the spirit and character of the people. It is they who will realize the promise and, hopefully, solve the problems in the years to come.

Shipboard portrait, Savannah, ca.1880. William Wilson photographer.

*Savannah? It's an amazing place. The dead, the
long-gone, people I never knew or loved, take
possession. Their houses are there, their parks, their
buildings of trade. Signaling themselves with bronze
markers and historical paragraphs. Nothing is mine. It
all belongs to a General Bull, Oglethorpe, or fancier
names I can't remember. I have no history there. So
explain it to me, if you can, why just walking her
streets, just feeling her warm bricks, just tasting the air
off her water can bring me closer to the home of my
being than any other place I know?*

Sisters Court after the wedding;
St. Johns Church coffee by the
Green-Meldrim House.

Savannah, preceding pages:
The Cotton Exchange;
The riverfront.

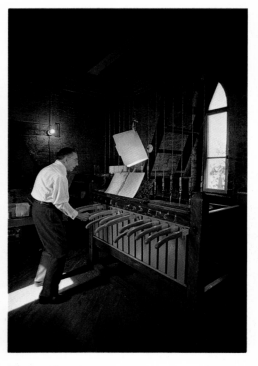

The resident jazz group;
The carillon player, St. Johns Church;
Dancer, Savannah Ballet.

Wormsloe: Just the drive to the house took you away.
It was not of any time we had ever known. This was
another place. Another consciousness. We sat in a
side room with the afternoon sun behind Mrs. Barrow's
head. She chose her position. She knew the glow.
We felt the drug of the sun. While that light
danced over and around her, like fairy lights on small
Peale miniatures, and tiny French masters and silver
snuff boxes with seals and crests, she told
us about riding ponies in the Pyrenees and eating
the heads of fish in Greece.

The Hugh Mercer House;
The Telfair Academy;
Train Number 1733, "The River Street
Rambler";
Garden, the Owens-Thomas House;
Archway of live oaks, Bay Street.

Preceding page: "Gingerbread House,"
Bull Street.

The stevedores were a great disappointment. They are huge men and have wondrous arms. Some are black and most have an "ethnic" look. But there they are, out on the water, the sky blue, the gulls screaming, the water thumping against the sides of huge foreign freighters, and they go about their work with the same expressions worn by secretaries dialing "information." I guess I expected them to sing. There's no romance in unloading beef from Argentina. Everyone says it's the fault of the union.

The port of Savannah:
Tugboat crewman;
Stevedore;
Docking.

*There's an art to picking crabs—
particularly with any speed to it.
Once you get in, you have to know
what you're after. The "Devil's
Fingers" can kill a man. You go
through a lot of mess to get a little
good. But folks pay like it's worth it.*

White shrimp, Brunswick;
Blue crabs, near Savannah;
Picking and packing crabmeat, near
Savannah;
Wassaw Island oyster beds;
Spoil bank by Steamboat Cut,
near Ossabaw Sound.

50

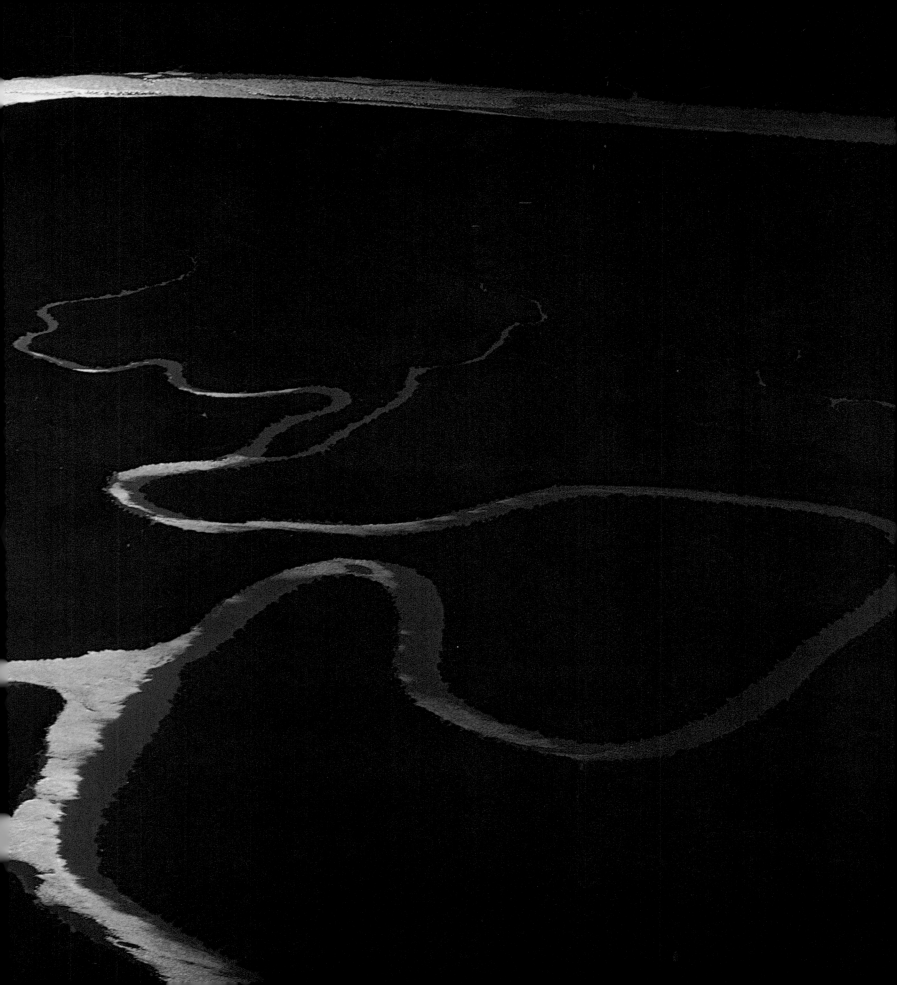

Wild iris, Cohutta Wilderness Area;
Azaleas and wisteria, Coffee Bluff;
Mushroom, Sylvania;
Cabbage palm, Wassaw Island;
Violets, Cohutta Wilderness Area;
Black-eyed susans, Foxfire Ridge;
Pink dogwood, Callaway Gardens.

Preceding pages:
Shrimp boat at sea, off Brunswick;
Rivers winding their way to the sea,
behind Sapelo Island;
Wild azalea, Callaway Gardens.

Listen close. There is a beating, a hum, a rhythm to this place. Nature is, was, and ever shall be. The only hope for frail mankind is to listen and learn the very spirit of this place. To beat in harmony with it.

These are the places of the herons and cranes and black-crested egrets. Of the clapper rail, the hawk, the owl. Of the beaches where the black-footed animals come down at night to wait for the turtles. Of the fiddler crab, the blues, the squarebacks, and the periwinkle snail. Of plankton, oysters, shrimp, and clams. Of whole juveniles of fish that glow with phosphorous in the dark spartina grass. These are the places, neither all terrestrial, nor all marine, that never have and never will accept what can't survive.

White ibis, Sapelo Island;
Cypress knees, Okefenokee Swamp;
Swamp silhouettes, Okefenokee Swamp.

Preceding pages:
Phlox, near Ellijay;
Live oak, Wassaw Island.

See the Appaloosa on the
Hill, his spotted blanket mixing
With the sky. Know him
For the horse he is.
Remember him as the place the stars chose
To fall.

Country lines, near Pine Mountain;
Hay barn, near Candler.

Preceding pages:
Brown pelicans over the steaming ocean,
off Sapelo Island;
Billy's Lake, Okefenokee Swamp;
Appaloosas at sunrise, Wolf Fork Valley.

A small town can be very tolerant of a person's eccentricities, particularly if they are expressed specifically and simply. He once said he liked apples because they had no edges and dogs because they could not talk. He knew one man he respected, and that was because that man respected him.

Upper pasture, Tiger Mountain;
Freshly picked pears, near Blue Ridge.

Hot pint jars were lined up like a row of dark, glass beads on a stained towel. They held the jams. Jams thick with sugar and all the sweetness of an already-gone summer. Grape jams spiced with honey and cinnamon and cloves. Tomato preserves lacquered with limes and nutmeg. Conserves used only at Thanksgiving, Christmas, and Easter. Riddled with walnut meats, raisins, oranges, and brandy. Brown syrupy apple jam hoping for brown bread and butter and smelling of bourbon. Green peppers, hot and bell, were washed and ready for the pepper jelly. From India bells of enamel, and tin, and aluminum, the kitchen sounds rode the cotton-curtain breeze.

Hand-sewn blanket, near Tiger;
Homemade goodies for sale, Clayton;
Georgia products, near Alto.

Preceding page:
The watermelon market, Cordele.

Seeding time, near Tiger;
Feeding the cows, near Sylvester;
Mennonite farmer, near Montezuma;
Farm family, near Statesboro;
Mennonite family life, near Montezuma;
Farm family, near Sylvester;
A father's embrace, Cordele.

Preceding page:
Working in a sea of cabbages, near Dillard.

There are those men who can never articulate their love. They seem innocent of its very meaning. But who, in one bending, one hand-on-head, one almost brutish gesture, have given their children whole lifetimes of affection.

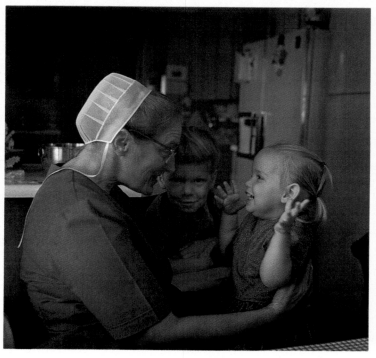

Tobacco warehouse, Metter;
Pecans, Albany;
Checking the harvest, near Sylvester;
Boiling peanuts, Hiawassee;
Sorting and packing apples, Tiger.

Preceding page:
Piglet, near Sylvester.

It might be tobacco, soybeans, peanuts,
whatever, but for a whole lot of people it's a living.
Far more than that, it's a way of life.

MEMBER

*In their very bending to the earth,
they seem to have risen above it. Like
wise but unknowing angels, they
float suspended in their simple tasks.*

Seeding the upper meadow, near Tiger;
Mennonite boy and his father,
near Montezuma.

Preceding page:
Church elder, near Savannah.

94

*Even the most close-mouthed
woman will reveal herself to you through the
conspiracy of snapping beans.*

Snapping beans at a fish camp,
Ogeechee River;
Snake handler, Hiawassee Mountain Fair;
Saturday-night bath, near Gainesville;
1080 rattlesnake rattles, Fargo;
Fish camp scene, Ogeechee River.

We've had our fair share of big men. Statesmen, a President, the head of Coca-Cola, some God-fearing, man-loving preachers, and even a poet or two. Imagine them all on some big, breezy porch, after a dinner of chicken and greens and.biscuits—and maybe a chess pie. Imagine them discussing their childhoods. It's their childhoods that they have in common. The names and the places are different, and you know the situations are bound to vary, but in the sounds and the smells and the very feelings, there has got to have been something akin. Therein lies the very promise of the still smallest, unknown child walking the streets of Newborn or Ty Ty, kicking a rock with a vengeful joy.

The gang, Gillsville;
Melon loader, Cordele;
Student, Fargo.

Atlanta delights in teasing your sense of time and place. You can ride an illuminated car into the white light of the sun, and stand fingertip-to-fingertip with a cloud; or you can pick pokeweed the entire length of Peachtree Street.

Elevators at the Omni;
First Methodist Church.

Preceding page:
Atlanta sunrise.

Construction on the new Coca-Cola
headquarters tower;
"Mr. Bob"—Robert W. Woodruff;
Coca-Cola research lab;
Inman railroad yards, Atlanta.

*A railroad sun is a different thing from a pasture sun,
or a highway sun, or the one that hangs over the sea. It
is that very most silver part of the sun that twists and
turns and reverses and glides in one long ribbon of a
gleam, peculiar only to railroad yards.*

Atlanta: Well, they come all right, and they just keep coming. Coming with a light shining in their eyes that rivals that of a pilgrim headed for Mecca. That's what it is anyway, a mecca. A great sparkling city beckoning to all to come and make it their religion. Make it their own.

It with its mysteries of shiny buildings—some made never-ending by the clouds that mask their finish and so, their reality. Glass tubes of structures that finger the sky and cheap-thrill the imagination with their neon space elevators. There's a lot of steel and concrete, and twice as much glass to reflect it all back to you triple-fold. It smacks of being brand new and just for you. It's knocked itself out to be like every other big city you've ever been to, and at the same time it's not like any other city you can name. If you move there from L.A., it's different. If you come from Cleveland, it's different. Even if you grew up right smack in the middle of Peachtree Road, it's different because it refuses to remain the same. Just about the time you've figured out which way a street runs, they turn it around. Pick a favorite restaurant, and in three months they will have changed the name. Just about the time you've figured out the ritual, Atlanta changes the ceremony.

July Fourth parade, Peachtree Street;
The Atlanta Symphony in Piedmont Park;
Brass bands;
Official, Peachtree Marathon.

Preceding page:
Calling the bet, Grant Park.

The plunge, Athens;
Football spectators on a rainy
Saturday, Athens;
Georgia Tech majorette, Atlanta;
Bulldog battle prayer, Athens.

Preceding pages:
Reception at the Swan House, Atlanta;
Gospel singing in the Omni.

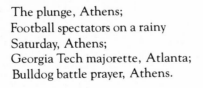

A sport is a game or contest requiring some degree of skill, and usually some physical exercise. While sporting participants are frequently described poetically, poetry is never recognized as a sport. They both depend on luck and magic. Either way that makes it hard to be a winner.

Callaway Gardens—Before the race,
The slalom event.

The Masters could easily be described only in terms of azaleas, dogwoods, alpaca sweaters and good whiskey. That wouldn't be fair. That would be disrespectful to a survived Depression, one World War, and some others with no names. That would be disrespectful to a man named Robert T. Jones, Jr., a creek named Rae's, and a 77-year-old man named Gene Sarazen. During the Tournament he sits in knickers on the clubhouse porch. The people who stop to speak to him know how in 1935, on the Par 5, 485-yard-long, 15th, he tied for first place in the last round by holing out of his second shot with a 4 wood for a double eagle 2. He went on to win the playoff, consequently the Masters, and one green jacket. That's where respect begins, and enough respect makes a tradition.

Tailgate party, the Masters;
Time-honored hat;
Official, the Masters;
Arnold Palmer.

Preceding page:
The Masters, Augusta.

We plant watermelons around mid-April. Toward the end of July they start coming in. The Charleston Grey is the first, then all of them—the Congo, Cannonball, Sugar Baby, the old Tom Watson, even the yellow ones like the Golden Honey. Some folks claim the yellow ones are better than all the rest. Unnerving as the color might be. There's the planting and the tending, but the real skill comes in the seed spitting. A good melon is actually nothing more than some sweet sugar water and some seeds for spitting. Children learn seed spitting from cousins or silly adults on back porches. Sometimes in the dead of winter you will find a seed that's been stuck to a piece of lattice stripping for whole seasons of summers. You don't start counting just how far you can spit a watermelon seed until you've well passed 20 feet. It takes a lot of practice. Only a few have the natural skill. Your height or that of the porch doesn't really seem to matter.

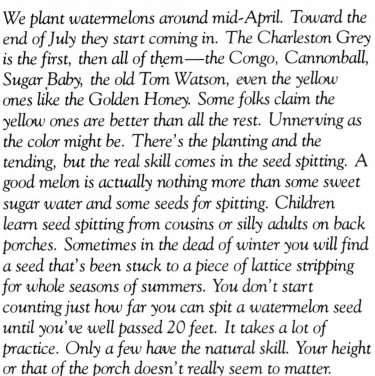

Cordele:
Judging the Watermelon Taste Contest;
Watermelon Festival parade;
Big melon, big bite;
Future watermelon men;
Present and future watermelon queens.

Detroit did a terrible thing to womankind when it invented the car. Because a man who truly loves cars never really loves a woman. Not the way she wants anyway. One way or another the woman loses out. There's just more shine about a car. He can start off with something as simple as a few chrome jobs, like pipes or mags, but by the time he has gotten into heavier stuff like 72 coats of metal-flake lacquer, well then, a whole new set of priorities has taken over. A veritable idol of a thing has happened. The graven image has come. Once more man has created himself a religion. But this one's good for 185 miles per hour.

Before the race, Road Atlanta,
Chestnut Mountain;
The classic look, Helen.

You don't forget the woman who bore you, and you don't forget the man who taught you to hunt. To forget either would be as unnatural as forgetting your own name. When you get to be a man, you thank both of them for breathing the life into you.

Retrieving the bird, Sylvania;
The hunting lodge after the hunt, Sylvania;
The plantation hunting wagon, Albany.

There are countrysides, banks, faces, mountains, gorges, whole rivers of rock, to remind us always of the earth. Of something bigger, harder, greater. Ready to thrust through and be known at any time.

Bank Fishing, Ogeechee River;
Section Four, Chattooga River,
near Clayton.
Following pages:
Daybreak, Okefenokee Swamp;
The final plunge, Callaway Gardens.

I am the geography of my place.
Like it I always have been.
I always will be. I am, that I am.

THE AUTHORS

Dick Durrance II

Born in Atlanta in 1943, photographer Bill Weems has always considered Georgia to be his home place. He has traveled extensively throughout the state in recent years, and during those trips he took the photographs that appear in this book.

Mr. Weems, who holds an M.A. in international economics and law, has worked as a foreign policy analyst, a legislative assistant to a U.S. Senator, a Navy photographer and a TV cameraman. He became a professional freelance photographer in 1975, and since then his work has appeared in *National Geographic, Fortune, Business Week, Southern Living* and many other national magazines and newspapers. His photographs have also been used by the Associated Press and the CBS television show *60 Minutes,* and he is a frequent contributor to books and multi-media shows. He was the main color photograph contributor to the book, *The Bicentennial Portrait of the American People,* and his photographs have been included in shows at the Kennedy Center and other galleries in the Washington, D.C., area. Currently he specializes in corporate and advertising photography, as well as editorial photographic coverage.

Mr. Weems now lives in Washington, D.C., with his wife, Prisca Crettier, his 11-year-old son, Will, and his 9-year-old daughter, Prisca.

Judy Z. Allen is a writer, film director, copywriter and teacher who has always lived in rural Georgia. Her writings have appeared in *Southern Living, Pride, Atlanta* and several other magazines, and her column, "Blackberry Almanac", has been featured in *Georgia* magazine.

A former producer-director at NET in Athens, Georgia, Ms. Allen has written several radio and television scripts, including NET specials on St. Augustine, Florida, and Stone Mountain, Georgia. She has won several awards for her advertising copy.

Ms. Allen teaches art and English in Milledgeville, Georgia, where she lives with her 9-year-old daughter, Jodie.

Louis De Vorsey, Jr. is a professor of geography at The University of Georgia.

A historical geographer, he received his Ph.D. in 1965 from the University of London. He joined the Department of Geography of The University of Georgia in 1967 and then served as its Head from 1970-1972.

In 1975 he was awarded the Association of American Geographers' "Citation for Meritorious Contributions to the Field of Geography." He received an American Council of Learned Societies Fellowship to conduct research in English archives for 12 months during 1978-79.

Among Dr. De Vorsey's scholarly works are books entitled *The Indian Boundary in the Southern Colonies, 1763-1776* (1966) and *DeBrahm's Report of the General Survey in the Southern District of North America* (1971).

Under contract by the Georgia Office of Planning and Budget, Dr. De Vorsey is currently researching the historical geography of the Georgia-South Carolina boundary dispute under litigation in the United States Supreme Court.

ACKNOWLEDGMENTS

I am deeply indebted to a great number of people for their encouragement and support during the creation and production of this book. First off, without the National Geographic Society I never would have been able to take these photographs. Much of the material contained within these pages was shot while I was on assignment for *National Geographic* magazine, and I am grateful to have had the opportunity to cover the land and people of Georgia.

Mr. Bennett Brown, president, The Citizens and Southern National Banks of Georgia, also deserves a very special measure of thanks. It was Mr. Brown who recognized the desirability of reproducing these photographs in book form so that everyone in the state might have the opportunity to see them. Thus, with the financial assistance of The Citizens and Southern National Banks statewide, the production of this book was made possible.

I would also like to thank The Coca-Cola Company for the generous financial support and assistance that was so important to the production of the book.

Great personal appreciation is also extended to the following individuals, who not only urged me on, but made resources and personnel available to me in my quest to reach into all corners of Georgia:

Governor George Busbee, and the many state officials and civil servants who were so willing and generous with their help in the field;

Penn Worden, Jr., his wife, Nina, and Ernst Davis of the Georgia Chamber of Commerce, and the many members of the Chamber throughout the state;

Dr. Bob Anderson, vice president for research at The University of Georgia, Lee Anderson and The University of Georgia faculty and staff members statewide, especially those in the Agricultural Research Service. A special word of appreciation is due Bob Anderson for his unflagging support.

The list of the other people who assisted me at various stages of my coverage is long, and I fear that I shall unintentionally omit someone. If this occurs, I ask to be forgiven the oversight. I would like to offer heartfelt thanks to the following:

John Riggall, Charlene Murphy, Bucky Bowles, Larry Griffeth, Tina Carlson-Griffeth, Bruce Dell, Milton Folds, Ed Spivia, Joe Tanner, Tom Perdue, Joe Courson, Beth and Scott Glass, Mary Alexander, Gary Ford, Bill and Butch Crunkleton and family, Dennis Yaschik, Don Greene, Anthony Tortorici, Carlton Curtis, Billie Mitzner, Harold and Janet Carter, Dick and Joyce Murlless, John Crawford, Kathy Sakas and the entire Wilderness Southeast staff, Walker and Bonnie Montgomery, Carolyn Bryson, Jill Van Dresser-Cally and the Peachtree Plaza Hotel, Holly Miller, Charlotte Lovell, Wilber Maney, Buford Withrow, Ed Cooper, Hardy Johnson, Niel Wood and family, Ben Tucker, Ken and Arlene Clark, Lloyd and Viola Swartzentruber and family, Kim Tomlinson, Peter Hudson, Karen Barr, Ober Tyus, Werner and Lisa Bludaus, Sandy West, Carole Kismaric, Chuck Mikolaycak, Karen Keeney, Steve Uzzell, Dick Durrance, Cathy Doxit-Pratt, Kay Dixon and Woody Camp.

My greatest measure of appreciation is for my family— Prisca, Will and lil' Prisca—whose cheerful voices and words of encouragement came to me in roadside phone booths all over the state.

THE PHOTOGRAPHS

All of the photographs in this book, with the exception of "The final plunge" on page 134, were taken with Nikon F2 35mm SLR camera bodies. "The final plunge" was shot with a Nikonos III 35mm body. Below is a list of the other equipment used in taking these photographs.

1	The Post Office: 35mm f/1.4 Nikkor, 1 sec @ f/2.8, K 64, tripod.
2-3	The Boneyard: 24mm f/2.8 Nikkor-N, 1/90 sec @ f/2.8, K 64, tripod.
4-5	The outer pasture: 80-200mm f/4.5 Zoom-Nikkor, 1/125 sec @ f/11, K 64, panned.
6-7	Storm light: 24mm f/2.8 Nikkor, 1/125 sec @ f/5.6, K 64.
8-9	Checking the crops: 15mm f/5.6 Nikkor, 1/15 sec @ f/16, K 64.
10-11	The swimming hole: 24mm f/2.8 Nikkor-N, 1/125 sec @ f/8, K 64.
12-13	Sunrise on the beach: 80-200mm f/4.5 Zoom-Nikkor, 1/125 sec @ f/8-11, K 64.
14-15	Skyline: 500mm, f/8 Reflex-Nikkor-C, 1/60 sec @ f/8, K 64, tripod.
37	The Cotton Exchange: 24mm f/2.8 Nikkor-N, 1/125 sec @ f/11-16, K 64.
38-39	The riverfront: 80-200mm f/4.5 Zoom-Nikkor, 1/60 sec @ f/4.5, K 64, tripod.
40-41	Sisters Court: 35mm f/1.4 Nikkor, 1/125 sec @ f/2.8-4. Church coffee: 24mm f/2.8 Nikkor-N, 1/125 sec @ f/11, K 64.
42-43	Jazz group: 24mm f/2.8 Nikkor-N, 1/125 sec @ f/5.6, K 64. The carillon: 35mm f/1.4 Nikkor, 1/60 sec @ f/4, K 64. Dancer: 35mm f/1.4 Nikkor, 1/30 sec @ f/2, EPT 160.
44-45	The "Gingerbread House": 24mm f/2.8 Nikkor-N, 1/125 sec @ f/4, K 64.
46-47	The Hugh Mercer House: 180mm f/2.8 Nikkor-P, 1/125 sec @ f/11, K 64. The Telfair Academy: 24mm f/2.8 Nikkor-N, 1/125 sec @ f/11-16, K 64. Train Number 1733: 24mm f/2.8 Nikkor-N, 1/125 sec @ f/5.6, K64. Garden: 24mm f/2.8 Nikkor-N, 1/125 sec @ f/8-11, K 64. Archway: 80-200mm f/4.5 Zoom-Nikkor, 1/125 sec @ f/5.6-8, K 64.
48-49	Tugboat crewman: 24mm f/2.8 Nikkor-N, 1/125 sec @ f/5.6, K 64. Stevedore: 80-200mm f/4.5 Zoom-Nikkor, 1/90 sec @ f/4.5, K 64. Docking: 80-200mm f/4.5 Zoom-Nikkor, 1/125 sec @

f/8-11, K 64, tripod.

50-51 White shrimp: 50mm f/1.4 Nikkor-S, 1/125 sec @ f/11-16, K 64.
Blue crabs: 35mm f/1.4 Nikkor, 1/125 sec @ f/11, K 64.
Picking crabmeat: 35mm f/1.4 Nikkor, 1/15 sec @ f/1.4, K 64.
Oyster beds: 24mm f/2.8 Nikkor-N, 1/125 sec @ f/4-5.6, K 64.
Spoil bank: 24mm f/2.8 Nikkor-N, 1/125 sec @ f/8-11, K 64.

52-53 Shrimp boat: 500mm f/8 Reflex-Nikkor-C, 1/250 sec @ f/16, K 64.

54-55 Rivers: 80-200mm f/4.5 Zoom-Nikkor, 1/250 sec @ f/8, K 64.

56-57 Wild azalea: 55mm f/3.5 Micro-Nikkor, 1/90 sec @ f/8-11, K 64.

58-59 Wild iris: 35mm f/1.4 Nikkor, 1/125 sec @ f/4, K 64.
Azaleas and wisteria: 35mm f/1.4 Nikkor, 1/125 sec @ f/5.6-8, K 64.
Mushroom: 35mm f/1.4 Nikkor, 1/60 sec @ f/2, K 64.
Cabbage palm: 35mm f/1.4 Nikkor, 1/125 sec @ f/4-5.6 K 64.
Violets: 35mm f/1.4 Nikkor, 1/125 sec @ f/5.6, K 64.
Black-eyed susans: 24mm f/2.8 Nikkor-N, 1/125 sec @ f/8, K 64.
Pink dogwood: 55mm f/3.5 Micro-Nikkor, 1/125 sec @ f/8, K 64, tripod.

60-61 Phlox: 24mm f/2.8 Nikkor-N, 1/125 sec @ f/2.8, K 64.

62-63 Live oak: 80-200mm f/4.5 Zoom-Nikkor, 1/125 sec @ f/11, K 64, tripod.

64-65 White ibis: 80-200mm f/4.5 Zoom-Nikkor, 1/125 sec @ f/5.6, K 64.
Cypress knees: 35mm f/1.4 Nikkor, 1/125 sec @ f/11, K 64.
Swamp silhouettes: 500mm f/8 Reflex-Nikkor-C, 1/250 sec @ f/8, K 64.

66-67 Brown pelicans: 80-200mm f/4.5 Zoom-Nikkor, 1/125 sec @ f/16, K 64.

68-69 Billy's Lake: 80-200mm f/4.5 Zoom-Nikkor, 1/125 sec @ f/4.5-5.6, K 64.

70-71 Appaloosa at sunrise: 80-200mm f/4.5 Zoom-Nikkor, 1/125 sec @ f/5.6-8, K 64.

72-73 Country lines: 24mm f/2.8 Nikkor-N, 1/60 sec @ f/8, K 64, tripod.
Hay barn: 80-200mm f/4.5 Zoom-Nikkor, 1/125 sec @ f/11, K 64.

74-75 Upper pasture: 80-200mm f/4.5 Zoom-Nikkor, 1/125 sec @ f/11-16, K 64.
Pears: 24mm f/2.8 Nikkor-N, 1/125 sec @ f/8-11, K 64.

76-77 The watermelon market: 80-200mm f/4.5 Zoom-Nikkor, 1/125 sec @ f/4-5.6, K 64.

78-79 Blanket: 35mm f/1.4 Nikkor, 1/125 sec @ f/2.8-4, K 64.
Homemade goodies: 35mm f/1.4 Nikkor, 1/125 sec @ f/4, K 64.

Georgia products: 24mm f/2.8 Nikkor-N, 1/125 sec @ f/11-16, K 64.

80-81 A sea of cabbages: 500mm f/8 Reflex-Nikkor-C, 1/125 sec @ f/11, K 64.

82-83 Seeding time: 24mm f/2.8 Nikkor-N, 1/125 sec @ f/2.8, K 64.
Feeding the cows: 24mm f/2.8 Nikkor-N, 1/125 sec @ f/8-11, K 64.
Mennonite farmer: 85mm f/1.8 Nikkor, 1/125 sec @ f/8-11, K 64.
Farm family, Statesboro: 24mm f/2.8 Nikkor-N, 1/125 sec @ f/4-5.6, K 64.
Mennonite family life: 35mm f/1.4 Nikkor, 1/60 sec @ f/2, K 64.
Farm family, Sylvester: 24mm f/2.8 Nikkor-N, 1/125 sec @ f/8, K 64.
Father's embrace: 80-200mm f/4.5 Zoom-Nikkor, 1/125 sec @ f/4.5-5.6, K 64.

84-85 Piglet: 80-200mm f/4.5 Zoom-Nikkor, 1/125 sec @ f/4.5, K 64.

86-87 Tobacco warehouse: 35mm f/1.4 Nikkor, 1/30 sec @ f/2, K 64.
Pecans: 50mm f/1.4 Nikkor-S, 1/125 sec @ f/2, K 64.
Peanut crop: 24mm f/2.8 Nikkor-N, 1/125 sec @ f/8, K 64.
Boiling peanuts: 24mm f/2.8 Nikkor-N, 1/125 sec @ f/5.6-8, K 64.
Sorting apples: 24mm f/2.8 Nikkor-N, 1/60 sec @ f/4, EDP 200, FL-D filter.

88-89 Cotton harvest: 24mm f/2.8 Nikkor-N, 1/125 sec @ f/16, K 64.

90-91 Church elder: 24mm f/2.8 Nikkor-N, 1/125 sec @ f/5.6, K 64.

92-93 Seeding: 80-200mm f/4.5 Zoom-Nikkor, 1/125 sec @ f/11-16, K 64.
Mennonite boy: 35mm f/1.4 Nikkor, 1/30 sec @ f/2, K 64.

94-95 Snapping beans: 24mm f/2.8 Nikkor-N, 1/125 sec @ f/5.6-8.
Snake handler: 24mm f/2.8 Nikkor-N, 1/60 sec @ f/4, K 64.
Bath: 24mm f/2.8 Nikkor-N, 1/125 sec @ f/4, K 64.
Rattlesnake rattles: 80-200mm f/4.5 Zoom-Nikkor, 1/125 sec @ f/5.6, K 64, tripod.
Camp scene: 24mm f/2.8 Nikkor-N, 1/125 sec @ f/11-16, K 64.

96-97 The gang: 24mm f/2.8 Nikkor-N, 1/125 sec @ f/11-16, K 64.
Melon loader: 80-200mm f/4.5 Zoom-Nikkor, 1/125 sec @ f/5.6-8, K 64.
Student: 35mm f/1.4 Nikkor, 1/125 sec @ f/2.8-4, K 64.

98-99 Atlanta sunrise: 24mm f/2.8 Nikkor-N, 1/125 sec @ f/2.8, K 64.

100-101 The Omni: 20mm f/4 Nikkor, 1/60 sec @ f/4, K 64.

First Methodist Church: 80-200mm f/4.5 Zoom-Nikkor, 1/125 sec @ f/11-16, K 64.

102-103   The State Capitol: 20mm f/4 Nikkor, 2 sec @ f/4, K 64, tripod.

104-105   Night in Atlanta: 24mm f/2.8 Nikkor-N, 3 sec @ f/2.8, K 64, tripod.

106-107   Construction: 80-200mm f/4.5 Zoom-Nikkor, 1/125 sec @ f/8, K 64.
"Mr. Bob": 35mm f/1.4 Nikkor, 1/60 sec @ f/2.8-4, EPD 200, FL-D filter.
Coca-Cola lab: 35mm f/1.4 Nikkor, 1/60 sec @ f/2.8, EPD 200, FL-D filter.
Railroad yards: 35mm f/1.4 Nikkor, 1/250 sec @ f/8, K 64.

108-109   Grant Park: 24mm f/2.8 Nikkor-N, 1/125 sec @ f/8, K 64.

110-111   Parade: 24mm f/2.8 Nikkor-N, 1/125 sec @ f/8-11, K 64.
Atlanta Symphony: 24mm f/2.8 Nikkor-N, 1/60 sec @ f/2.8, K 64.
Brass bands: 80-200mm f/4.5 Zoom-Nikkor, 1/125 sec @ f/11-16, K 64.
Official: 80-200mm f/4.5 Zoom-Nikkor, 1/125 sec @ f/5.6-8, K 64.

112-113   Reception: 35mm f/1.4 Nikkor, 1/125 sec @ f/4-5.6, K 64.

114-115   Gospel singing: 15mm f/5.6 Nikkor-QD-C, 1/60 sec @ f/5.6, K 64.

116-117   The plunge: 80-200mm f/4.5 Zoom-Nikkor, 1/125 sec @ f/5.6, K 64.
Spectators: 24mm f/2.8 Nikkor-N, 1/125 sec @ f/5.6, K 64.
Majorette: 80-200mm f/4.5 Zoom-Nikkor, 1/125 sec @ f/11-16, K 64.
Battle prayer: 24mm f/2.8 Nikkor-N, 1/125 sec @ f/5.6, K 64.

118-119   Before the race: 80-200mm f/4.5 Zoom-Nikkor, 1/125 sec @ f/5.6, K 64.
The slalom: 400mm f/5.6 Nikkor-PC, 1/250 sec @ f/8, K 64.

120-121   The Masters: 80-200mm f/4.5 Zoom-Nikkor, 1/125 sec @ f/8-11, K 64.

122-123   Tailgate party: 24mm f/2.8 Nikkor-N, 1/125 sec @ f/2.8-4, K 64.
Time-honored hat: 35mm f/1.4 Nikkor, 1/125 sec @ f/11-16, K 64.
Official: 80-200mm f/4.5 Zoom-Nikkor, 1/125 sec @ f/11-16, K 64.
Arnold Palmer: 35mm f/1.4 Nikkor, 1/125 sec @ f/11-16, K 64.

124-125   The Watermelon Contest: 24mm f/2.4 Nikkor-N, 1/125 sec @ f/2.8-4, K 64.
Watermelon parade: 80-200mm f/4.5 Zoom-Nikkor, 1/125 sec @ f/5.6, K 64.

Big bite: 35mm f/1.4 Nikkor, 1/125 sec @ f/2.8-4, K 64.
Future watermelon men: 24mm f/2.8 Nikkor-N, 1/125 sec @ f/5.6, K 64.
Watermelon queens: 16mm f/3.5 Fisheye-Nikkor, 1/125 sec @ f/11-16, K 64.

126-127   Road Atlanta: 80-200mm f/4.5 Zoom-Nikkor, 1/125 sec @ f/11-16, K 64.
The classic look: 80-200mm f/4.5 Zoom-Nikkor, 1/125 sec @ f/11-16, K 64.

128-129   Retrieving the bird: 35mm f/1.4 Nikkor, 1/125 sec @ f/2, K 64.
After the hunt: 24mm f/2.8 Nikkor-N, 1/90 sec @ f/5.6, K 64.
The hunting wagon: 24mm f/2.8 Nikkor-N, 1/125 sec @ f/8, K 64.

130-131   Bank fishing: 80-200mm f/4.5 Zoom-Nikkor, 1/125 sec @ f/4.5-5.6, K 64.
Section Four: 80-200mm f/4.5 Zoom-Nikkor, 1/250 sec @ f/8-11, K 64.

132-133   Daybreak: 80-200mm f/4.5 Zoom-Nikkor, 1/30 sec @ f/4.5, K 64.

134   The final plunge: 35mm f/2.8 Nikkor, 1/250 sec @ f/11, K 64.

Custom prints of all photographs in this book are available. Please write Ms. Katie Phelps, The Phelps Agency, 32 Peachtree Street, N.W., Atlanta, Georgia 30303.